BEST LOVED
POEMS
of KOREA

BEST LOVED
POEMS
of KOREA

SELECTED
FOR FOREIGNERS

Translated by Chang-soo Ko

HOLLYM

First published in 1984
Seventh printing, 1998
by Hollym International Corp.
18 Donald Place, Elizabeth, New Jersey 07208 USA
Phone: (908) 353-1655   Fax: (908) 353-0255
http:/www.hollym.com

Published simultaneously in Korea
by Hollym Corporation; Publishers
13-13 Kwanchol-dong, Chongno-gu,
Seoul 110-111, Korea
Tel: (02)735-7554   Fax: (02)730-8192
http://www.hollym.co.kr

ISBN: 0-930878-35-3
Library of Congress Catalog Card Number: 83-81485

Printed in Korea

CONTENTS

PART THREE

INTRODUCTION

It is hoped that the present volume gives some idea about modern Korean poetry in terms of subject matter, themes and modes of expression. The majority of the poems have been taken from among the most widely read and best-loved poems. The present book, however, cannot claim to present a satisfactory cross-section of modern Korean poetry. Among other things, the poems presented in the volume were chosen largely on the basis of the degree to which individual poems rendered themselves to translation into the English language and partly on the basis of the personal preferences of the translator.

As may conceivably be the case with most translations of poetry, it is extremely difficult, if not entirely impossible, to put into another language the musical and lyrical qualities of the original poems without seriously damaging their beauty. For that reason, many good poems fail to be translated, or included in anthologies such as this. The translator tried to be faithful, as far as possible, to a literal, word-by-word translation in the belief that, while elements like rhythms and other sound devices are largely lost in translation, imagery best survives translation into another language and transcends linguistic and cultural boundaries.

Korean poetry has a long history spanning many centuries and has had various verse forms at different periods of time. Poetry has been very close to the Korean heart. The Koreans have greatly loved poetry as a medium for expressing their thoughts and feelings. Whether in sorrow or in joy, they have turned to poetry. They have also been endowed with extraordinary poetic talents.

The Shilla Dynasty had Hyangga poetry which flourished between the 7th and 10th centuries A.D. The Koryo Dynasty had its own verse forms, often called Koryo songs (10th-14th centuries) and Kyonggi songs (13th-16th centuries). The Yi Dynasty produced a considerable amount of poetry in the form of Royal odes (15th century) and Kasa songs (15th-19th centuries). The Yi Dynasty also saw the florescence of Sijo poems. A short, epigrammatic verse of three lines, Sijo was the first vernacular verse in the true sense of the word in Korean poetic history and made its advent following the creation of Korea's unique phonetic alphabet in the 15th century. Among these traditional verse forms, Sijo has probably influenced the style of modern Korean poetry most, and Sijo writing is perhaps largest in bulk.

Apart from these poetic genres, it must be pointed out that there is a treasury of poetry written by Koreans in Chinese characters and a wealth of Buddhist poetry. The bulk of these poems remains virtually untapped.

Korean poetry as a whole is marked by the love of and intimacy with Nature. A cursory look at Korean poetry, old and new, suffices to show that the majority of poems deal with themes related to Nature. A nostalgic and affectionate attitude towards Nature is conspicuous among a large number of Korean poems. This attitude to Nature perhaps harks back to the world-views of Buddhism, Confucianism and Taoism, which have profoundly influenced the Korean ways of life and thinking. Korea has also had hermetic traditions in which the poet retired to the countryside as an escape from the mundane world and in search of the Way. In a way, Nature represented incarnations of the Way, Heaven and Eternity. The Korean poet reacts sensitively to subtle changes in Nature, the different seasons and the times of the day. He also seems to be acutely mindful of the transience of human life. The Korean poet has thus drawn much inspiration from Nature. All these things will be immediately noticeable in the poems introduced in the present anthology.

In the more recent decades, particularly following the Korean War, the embittered poet has turned more and more to day-to-day, practical aspects of life and the human condition in modern, urban settings. For he could not remain untouched by the occurrences in this turbulently changing world. His interests and concerns both as poet and man have inevitably altered in character and scope. In fact, his concerns seem to cover the whole spectrum of issues that confront modern man.

Naturally, in modern Korean poetry, traditional poetic form and content become less and less discernible. Korean idiosyncrasies seem to diminish under the influx of outside influences and the rapid changes in life style and thinking. These things notwithstanding, one notes that what can best be termed typical Korean patterns of thought, feeling and expression persist in poetry.

It appears to me that the Korean poet has ably given expression to the sorrows and joys of his fellow countrymen. He has successfully interwoven Korean sensibility into his poetic language. The Korean poet has indeed importantly contributed to purifying and enriching his mother tongue.

PART ONE

SPRING RAIN

A low and quiet voice calls.
I go outdoors, ah, I go outdoors.
Milky, slumbrous clouds,
Heavy and slow,
Drift across the blue sky.
Ah, my inexplicable forlornness!

A low and quiet voice calls.
I go outdoors, ah, I go outdoors.
Like dim memories of past days,
Tremulous and invisible flower-breath
Is so fragrant.
Ah, my inexplicable heart-ache!

A low and quiet voice calls.
I go outdoors, ah, I go outdoors.
No trace of milky clouds
Or flower-breath;
Only the spring rain falls,
Fine as silver-threads,
Quiet as pensive care.
Ah, I am waiting in vain!
                    by Yung-ro Byun

MY MIND

My mind is a lake.
Please come in your boat.
Clasping your white shadow,
I'll shatter like jade
Against the bow.

My mind is a candle-light.
Please close that door.
I'll quietly burn to the last drop,
Flickering by your silken dress.

My mind is a wanderer.
Please play on that flute.
Listening in the moonlight,
I'll be awake all the night-tide.

My mind is a dead leaf.
Please let me stay briefly in your garden.
When the wind rises again,
I'll leave you, lonely as a wanderer.

by Dong-myung Kim

SOME DAY

If some day you come back,
Then I'll say, "I've forgot."

If you blame me at heart,
"I've forgot after much longing."

If you still chide me,
"I've forgot, I couldn't trust."

"I've forgot,"
Not today or tomorrow,
But "some day."

by So-wol Kim

ROCK

When I die,
I will become a rock,
never touched
by compassion, joy or anger.
While being torn down by wind and rain,
It will only whip itself inwards
in eternal, impersonal silence,
and at last forget its own existence;
Floating clouds, distant thunder!

Though it may dream,
it will never sing.
Though broken in pieces,
it will never utter a word.
I will become such a rock.

by Chi-hwan Yu

FLOWER PETALS ON THE SLEEVES

The sky far away
Above cold mountain-rocks.
Wild birds
Cry mournfully.

The clouds flow
A thousand miles down the river.

The wanderer's long sleeves
Are wet from flower petals.
Twilight over a riverside village
Where wine is mellow.

When this night is over,
Flowers will fall in that village.

The heart is sad and tender
    to a fault.
The wanderer goes,
Drifting quietly in the moonlight.

by Ji-hoon Cho

I DO NOT KNOW

Whose footprint is that paulonia leaf
That drops softly, rousing ripples in the windless air?
Whose face is that blue sky
Glimpsed between the threatening, dark clouds
Blown by the west wind after a long rain?

Whose breath is that fragrance in the sky
Over the flowerless tree, over the old tower?
Whose song is that bickering stream
That quietly flows, starting from nowhere
And making the stones weep?
Whose poem is that evening glow
That adorns the fading day,
Its lotus feet standing on the endless sea,
And its jade hands patting the sky?

Burnt ashes become fuel again.
My endlessly burning heart,
Whose night does this
Flickering lamp illumine?

                              by Yong-woon Han

SNOW FALLS

Snow falls
On this winter morning.

That snow is so white
And its sound so still;
I shall bow my head and pray.

Sadness shades your lips, Beloved!
Do you too love that snow?

Snow falls;
It's time to pray together.
by Jang-hi Lee

DEER

The long neck makes him a sad creature,
Always gentle and quiet.
The fragrant crown betrays
His noble birth.

Looking at his image
Reflected in the stream,
He recalls the lost myths,
Then in helpless nostalgia,
Cranes the sad neck
To gaze at far-away hills.

by Chun-myung No

AZALEA FLOWERS

When you hate to see me
And decide to leave,
I'll quietly let you go.

I'll pluck an armful of azaleas
In the *Yaksan* hills at *Yungbyun*
To strew over your path.
Tread softly on the flowers,
Each step soft and silent.

When you hate to see me
And decide to leave,
I'll never, never shed tears.
                    by So-wol Kim

REED FLUTE

I play a reed flute
On a Spring's hill,
Longing for old home.

I play a reed flute
On a blooming hill,
Longing for childhood days.

I play a reed flute
In human streets,
Longing for earthly things.

I play a reed flute
On an endless wandering
Over the vales of tears.
                    by Ha-woon Han

GASLIGHT

A gaslight hangs in the empty sky;
Where does this sad signal direct me?

The long summerday hastily folds its wings.
The skyscrapers stand in the twilight like pale tombstones.

The glaring night is dishevelled like weeds
And thoughts have lost their speech.

The darkness soaks the skins.
The noise in strange streets
Saddens me inexplicably.

Mingling in the vain crowds,
From where have I brought this heavy sorrow?
My long shadow is thick dark.

Were does this sad signal direct me?
A gaslight hangs in the empty sky.

by Kwang-kyun Kim

GRAPES

July in my native village
Arrives in mellow grapes.

Then the legends of this village
Yield their fruit in clusters,
And the distant sky, dreaming,
Comes into each grape.

When the blue sea under the sky
Bares her hidden bosom,
And a ship with white sails
Comes gently shoving,

The guest I await will arrive
With a blue robe over his weary person.

If he shares the grapes on my table,
I do not mind wetting my hands.

Boy, get ready on the table
A silver plate and a ramie napkin.
                    by Yuk-sa Lee

BESIDE CHRYSANTHEMUMS

Perhaps to bring a chrysanthemum to bloom
The cuckoo has been crying
So loud since springtime.

Perhaps to bring a chrysanthemum to flower
The thunder roared so in the dark clouds.

A flower that resembles my elder sister,
Who now stands before her mirror,
Back from the hidden lanes of her distant youth
Where love and longing pained her heart so.

Perhaps for your yellow flowers to bloom
We had the first frost last night,
And I lay sleepless all night long.

by Jung-ju Suh

BLOSSOM

A blossom drops from the tree
Through the windless air.
I pick it up and hold it on the palm
To give it a better glance.
Petals shiver in the warmth;
The pollen flies away.
When I call "flower!"
It falls off my hand and
Drops somewhere to an unknown depth.
Now a nameless thing comes
And silently perches on the fringe of the tree.

by Chun-soo Kim

WANDERER

Over the ferry,
Along the corn-field path,

A wanderer goes
As the moon
In the clouds.

A single road stretches
A thousand miles southward.

Twilight over a riverside village
Where wine is mellow.

The wanderer goes
As the moon
In the clouds.

by Mok-wol Park

TILL PEONIES BLOOM

Till peonies bloom,
I shall be waiting for my spring.
When peonies have all fallen,
Then shall I mourn for the lost spring.

On a May day, a hot summer day,
Even the fallen petals withered;
No peony could be seen anywhere in the world,
And my towering hope sadly crumbled.

With the falling of peonies my year ends.
I weep away the rest of the year.
Till peonies bloom,
I shall still be waiting
For the spring of glorious sorrow.

by Yung-rang Kim

CANNOT FORGET

You will remember
'cause you cannot forget.
Let a lifetime pass
As it is, as it is.
Someday you'll forget.

You will remember
'cause you cannot forget.
Let the seasons flow
As it is, as it is.
You'll forget some,
If not all.

"When Love makes me remember,
How shall I ever forget?"
                                    by So-wol Kim

DAYTIME SLUMBER

The mother takes a sweet slumber,
Clasping the sleeping baby's hand.
A drowsy midday.

The baby's face glows
Like the fair moon
Floating on the lake.
The round eyes, open or closed,
Illumine the room.

A bunch of tiny flowers
Or a basketful of mellow fruit;
The baby emits warm skin smell,
The baby's fresh fragrance.

Mother and baby
Are in communion even in sleep;
Shall I call it an echo riding
On a golden chariot?
Or a Spring wind kissing green buds?

When the baby opens its eyes,
The mother wakes, too.
When the baby smiles,
The mother's heart fills with sunlight.
                              by Nam-jo Kim

THE DEPARTING BOAT

I am leaving, too.
Shall I just pine away my youth?
I am also leaving.

Can I easily abandon
This sheltered haven?

Even in tears I can see
My beloved people.
I can even tell
The wrinkles on their faces
Like the well-trodden paths in the vale.

Whether one deserts or escapes,
It is painful to forget.
The winds are whipping the clouds.
There is no haven on the opposite bank.

I am leaving, too.
Shall I just pine away my youth?
I am also leaving.

by Yong-chul Park

FLAG

That soundless clamour.
Eternal Nostalgia's handkerchief
Fluttering toward the blue expanse.
Purity waves in the wind.
Sorrow spreads its wings like a heron
On that pure and straight pole of Ideal.
Who first hoisted that sad mind
  in the sky?
by Chi-hwan Yu

LONGING

What shall I do, Waves?
Waves, what shall I do?
Love is unmoved like the shore.
What shall I do, Waves?
What shall I do?
by Chi-hwan Yu

PART TWO

PART TWO

AZALEA FLOWERS

Azaleas are eaten in my native land.
The more you eat, the hungrier you get.

Drunken with the azaleas she'd eaten,
Suny would doze off with the basket in her arms.
Now one hears little about her.

The boy back from the big city
chews the azaleas
on a drowsy May's hill.

Azaleas are eaten in my native land.
The more you eat, the hungrier you get.

by Yun-hyun Cho

POEM OF THE OLD GARDEN

The night has swallowed the village.
The frog sounds have swallowed the night.
One, two, three...
The lamplight dashes through the frog sounds.

At last the drunkard moon
Sneaks out and vomits
A landscape painted in silver.

by Jong-han Kim

YELLOW GRAPE-LEAVES

On the dark, wet garden
fall quietly
yellow grape-leaves.
drop, drop, drop...

Today once more I weep
As I the dead leaves sweep.

When will this tragedy end?

On the dark, wet garden
fall quietly
yellow grape-leaves.
drop, drop, drop...
by Il-do O

MY MAIDEN

With her basket hung on a bare branch,
Where has my maiden gone?

The silky haze
Glimmers about the branch.
by Il-do O

SPRING DAY

The blue sea bares
Its white teeth
Between red camellia blossoms.

Waves shatter
By the window.

A yellow butterfly
Hovers around a glass vase,

Then recedes
Like a petal.

by Ji-hoon Cho

LONGING FOR HOME

Your sash
In the wheat field.

Your smell
In the wheat field.

We crawled like pheasants!

The skylark family flew away
From their nest in the wheat field.
That day we parted
In the wheat field.

In the wheat field,
In the wheat field!
                    by Sun-won Hwang

TO THE SUN'S ARMS

Look at the sun. Look at the rising, blazing sun.
When the sun once again rises over the hills,
let us go to the fresh, fragrant grass-fields.
Let us fare the dazzling morning's way toward the sun.
Drive away the darkness. Drive away the darkness
that howls like beasts. Let it flock to the cliff
like beasts. Let it flock to the cliff with sunlight
over its back.

Look! those wild flowers blooming with a pungent
fragrance. Those green leaves dancing and waving;
the bird songs like crystal beads; the blue water
racing down the valley; all the mountains rise anew
to embrace the light...

The green grass-leaves rustle; in the waving trees,
the leaves rustle; in the clear streamlet little
silver fish frolic; the stone splashes the water;
inchworms on the branches, ants below; they cry
hurrah in broad daylight! All the green things,
all the living things in all the hills reverberate,
echo, overwhelm in a chorus.

Mountains! blue mountains with fluttering leaves!
The morning with its spreading and leaping sunrays
pricks its ears for all the sounds; its eyes open
to the sunrays. My blood runs anew. All my body
vibrates. I am light as birds... Walking the green
morning's road... Walking toward the arms of the newly
rising sun.

by Du-jin Park

EVOCATION

A name shattered to pieces!
A name scattered in the void!
A name that never replies!
A name that I'll die calling!

The one word left in the soul
To the last I couldn't pronounce.
My beloved!
My beloved!

The red sun hovers over the hill,
And the deer moan woefully.
I'm calling your name
On a lonely hill.

I call your name in great sorrow,
I call your name in deep sorrow.
My voice reaches towards the sky,
But the sky is too far from the earth.

Turn me into stone,
I'll call your name till I die.
My beloved!
My beloved!

by So-wol Kim

LYRICISM

The rain was falling.
The winds hanging in the trees
Were tearing to pieces.

You were clinging to my arms.
The rain was also falling
In the back-lanes
Where the night was nearing.

In the rain-soaked darkness
Your hands hugged my face,
And then you asked
With a tender voice,
With a warm voice.
                    by Bong-gun Chun

SELF-PORTRAIT

All alone I visit a deserted well
by a paddy-field beyond the hill.
Then I quietly look into the water.

In the well, the moon is bright; clouds saunter;
the sky spreads; blue winds breathe; the autumn
dwells; and there is a man.

Somehow I hate the man. So I turn around to go away.
On my way back, I feel sorry for the man.

I return to the well and look down. He remains
in his place. I hate him again. I turn around to
go away. On the way back, I long for the man.

In the well, the moon is bright; clouds saunter;
the sky spreads; blue winds breathe; the autumn
dwells; and the man stands there like memory.

by Dong-ju Yun

SOUND OF RAIN

It is raining.
The night quietly spreads its feathers.
The rain murmurs in the garden
Like a chick lisping furtively.

The hazy moon became wan and
Warm winds began to breathe
As if the spring flowed from the sun.
And it is raining this dark night.

It is raining.
The rain arrives like a kind guest.
I open the window to receive him.
The rain falls, murmuring and unseen.

It is raining on the garden,
The window and the roof.
The rain falls,
Bringing secret glad **tidings** to my heart.

by Yo-han Chu

MIRROR

There is no sound in the mirror;
You will find no world so quiet.

I have ears in the mirror, too:
Two pitiful ears
That cannot understand my words.

I am left-handed in the mirror:
A left-hander who cannot
Shake hands with me or others.

I cannot touch myself in the mirror
Because of the mirror.
But how could I have ever met
Myself in the mirror
If it had not been for the mirror?

Though I have no mirrors anymore,
I remain always in the mirror.
Though I am not quite sure,
He is pre-occupied with left-handed projects.

The one in the mirror is my reversal
But resembles me very much, too.
I am sad because I cannot worry about
Or examine myself in the mirror.

by Sang Lee

OBEDIENCE

Others say they love freedom, but I love
obedience. Though I know freedom, I only
want to obey you. Willing obedience is
sweeter than just freedom. That is my bliss.

But if you tell me to obey some other person,
that I can never do.

For if I obey another person, I cannot obey you.

by Yong-woon Han

PLANE TREE

When I ask you, Plane Tree,
Whether you know how to dream,
Your hair floats in the blue sky.

Though you do not know love, Plane Tree,
You offer your own shade for others.

When I went a long, lonely way, Plane Tree,
You fared that path with me.

I want to breathe a soul
Deep into your roots, Plane Tree,
But I am not a God, either.

Is there in any distant corner, Plane Tree,
A patch of soil to receive you gladly
The day our thorny way ends?

I only want to watch over you
So you can be my good neighbour.

Beautiful stars shine and
My dear window is open on that path.

by Hyun-sung Kim

I'LL HAVE THE WINDOW SOUTHWARD

I'll have the window southward.
A piece of land will I have
To dig and weed with a hoe.

I'll never be lured by clouds.
I'll enjoy free bird songs.
When the corns are ripe,
Come and share them on my table.

When someone asks why I live,
I just smile.

by Sang-yong Kim

SMILE WAS MY ONLY FAULT

I only gave him
Directions for his road.
I only gave him a bowlful of water
I had drawn from the well.
I only smiled
'cause he thanked.
I don't care
If the sun doesn't rise
Over *Pyongyang* Castle.
The smile was
My only fault.

by Dong-hwan Kim

IT'S NOT YET TIME TO LIGHT THE CANDLES

The fine rays of the setting sun will complain;
Mother, do not light the candles yet.
The little birds of my meditation,
Are they not still winging in that blue sky?
At last the sky will become red like apples,
And those little birds will return with the dusk.
Our young sheep still lie on the old green couch,
    enjoying stray sunlight.

Now the evening fog settles down on the calm lake.
But, Mother, it's not yet time to light the candles.
The meditating face of the old mountain
    is not yet receding.
One cannot hear from the far-away forests
Night's footfalls or her dark trail rustling
    against her feet.

The faint sounds of the waves lapping distant shores
    gradually ebb away.
That's because the crows who visit the country
In late Autumn have gone far away with the winds.
Now on the mother's back the baby wants to sleep
    to the hummed lullaby.
Mother, do not yet light the candles.
Now in the sky over that forest,
A tiny star appears.

by Suk-jung Shin

THE WOODEN HORSE AND THE LADY

We drink a glass of wine
And talk of Virginia Woolf's life
And the garments of a lady
Who has gone on a wooden horse.
The wooden horse has departed into the autumn.
Tinkling its bells and leaving its owner behind.
A star falls from the wine bottle, and
The heart-broken star shatters against my heart.
A girl I knew for a time grows by garden plants.
Literature dies and life fades;
Even the truth of love forsakes
The shadows of love and hate.
Then you no more see the loved one on a wooden horse.
Seasons go to return in time.
So once we withered to avoid isolation
And now we must part;
Hearing the bottle fall in the wind,
We must look into the old authoress' eyes.
To the Lighthouse. . .
Though we can see no light, we must remember
The mournful sounds of the wooden horse
To save the future of pessimism we cherish.
Whether all parts or dies, somehow we must listen
To the sad tales told by Virginia Woolf,
Gripping the dim consciousness lingering in the mind.
Like a snake that has found its youth
After creeping between two rocks,
We must drink a glass of wine with open eyes.
For fear of what sorrow do we part,
When life is not lonely but
Commonplace as the cover of a magazine?
While the wooden horse is in the sky
With its bells tinkling at our ears;
While the fall wind moans hoarsely
In my fallen wine bottle.

by In-hwan Park

53

GOLDEN TURF

Turf, turf, golden turf!
The flames in the deep vale,
The golden turf o're Jane's tomb.

Spring splendour alights
On willow trees and
Slender boughs.

Spring splendour has come
To the golden turf
In the deep vale.
by So-wol Kim

MOTHER, SISTER

Mother, Sister! let's dwell by the river.
Gleaming golden sands in the garden.
Outside the back-gate, a chorus of reeds.
Mother, Sister! let's dwell by the river.
by So-wol Kim

MY MIND

My mind resembles calm lake-water
Rippled by stray winds,
Shadowed by flowing clouds.

Someone is throwing stones;
Another is fishing;
Another is singing.

By this shore on a lonely night,
Stars quietly float on the water
And the woods quietly lull the waves.

But each night I cover the lake with my dreams
Lest this shore be untidy
The day the white swan returns.
                    by Kwang-sup Kim

SUMMER MORNING AFTER A RAIN

After the rain stops,
The clear sky descends upon the pond
To usher in a summer morning.
Goldfish write poesy
On the green sheet.
                    by Kwang-sup Kim

THE SPRING IS A CAT

On a cat's fur soft as pollen,
The mild Spring's fragrance lingers.

In a cat's eyes round as golden bells,
The mad Spring's flame glows.

On a cat's gently closed lips,
The soft Spring's drowsiness lies.

On a cat's sharp whiskers,
The green Spring's life dances.
                    by Jang-hi Lee

THE CHIRPING CRICKET

The cricket that chirps here every night
Is chirping tonight under the floor.

The cricket sounds cold and dreary
As a stream that gleams at even-tide.

The cricket sound every night
Takes my soul prisoner.
                    by Jang-hi Lee

PART THREE

APRIL

A lone peak where
Pine pollen flies.

When a philomel bemoans
The long April day,

The forester's blind daughter
In her lone house

Puts her ears
On the paper door.
                    by Mok-wol Park

SEASHELL

The seashell is lonely
By the sea.

When forlorn
With futile hopes,
The seashell secretly
Longs for the depths.

As the seasons elapse,
The seashell's dreams
Harden by the sea water.

On the sea-shore
The seashell is lonely
All day, all night.

by Byung-hwa Cho

PLANTAIN

When did you leave your motherland?
The plantain's dreams are pitiful.

The burning nostalgia
For the South:
Your soul is lonelier
Than a nun.

A passionate lady,
When you long for rain.
I draw water from the well
To pour over your feet.

Now the night is cold,
I'll let you stay by my bed.
I'll gladly be your servant.

Let's warm our winter
With your long dress.
                    by Dong-myung Kim

MOUNTAIN PATH

1
I climb a mountain path,
Quiet and alone.
I climb a mountain path.

The sun has set,
Bird songs have ceased.
The footfalls of animals
Sound in the distance.

I climb a mountain path
Quiet and alone at night.
I climb a mountain path.

2
Silent night,
Dark forests.

The endless thick forests
Where one can see no stars.

The mountain path is rough,
The mountain path is endless.

3
There's a bonfire
On a dreamy mountain path.

(When will the mountain path end?)
(When will the dark night pass away?)

There's a bonfire
On a mountain rock.

by Ju-dong Yang

NIGHT

Night is
A lake shrouded in blue fog.

I am a fisherman
On a sleep's sail-boat,
Fishing dreams.
            by Dong-myung Kim

THE SEA TO THE BOY

I

Clash, roll, break!
I strike, I smash, I destroy:
Towering mountains, rocks big as houses.
I despise, I belittle, I roar.
Do you know my great strength?
I strike, I smash, I destroy.
Clash, roll, break, roar!

II

Clash, roll, break!
I have no fears.
Whoever wields power on earth
Is helpless before me.
Things, however big, are powerless
Before me, to me.
Clash, roll, break, roar!

III

Clash, roll, break!
Whoever has never knelt before me,
Let him step forward!
The Emperor of China, or Napoleon?
You too bend down before me.
Whoever can cope with me,
Let him challenge me!
Clash, roll, break, roar!

IV

Clash, roll, break!
Those who, in their tiny hills,
Islets or patches of land,
Pretend they are the only wise and holy ones,
Let them come and look at me!
Clash, roll, break, roar!

V

Clash, roll, break!
There is one equal for me:
That great, wide firmament,
He is indeed my kind.
He is free of petty grievances,
Conflicts or foul things,
Unlike the people in the mundane world.
Clash, roll, break, roar!

VI

Clash, roll, break!
I hate all the people in that world,
Except one group:
The brave and pure-hearted boys.
They snuggle up to me.
Come, my boys! I'll embrace you all.
Clash, roll, break, roar!

by Nam-sun Choe

EPITAPH AMONG SUNFLOWERS

Do not erect cold tombstones over my grave.
Plant yellow sunflowers about my grave.
Let me look out the endless cornfield
Between the sunflower stalks.

Think of the yellow sunflowers as my glorious love
That resembled the sun.

If you see skylarks
Shooting into the sky from the green cornfield,
Think of them as my soaring dreams.

by Hyung-soo Ham

PARTING

Shall I say I love her?
Then my heart yearns more.

Shall I leave, not seeing her,
But just this once more...

Ravens in the hills,
Ravens in the plain
Croak about the setting sun:
"She is setting o're the hills."

The river in the south,
The river in the north;
The flowing stream
Pulls and shoves,
Flowing ever on and on.
                    by So-wol Kim

ORDINARY AUTUMN EVENING

On an ordinary autumn evening
Ordinary fruit is better.
Sometimes ordinary words
With no peculiar savour
Suit me better.
Hearing in memory
The last car depart,
I step over
The membrane of sleep,
And a fruit falls in my dream.
I will ask the wind
That departs in the morning
To what depths the fruit has fallen.
by Dong-jip Shin

RAIN

When philomels sing in the April hills,
Rain arrives over the green turf.

Rain's eyes are clear as crystals.
Rain boasts a white pearl necklace.

Rain weaves silver lace all day long
In the shade of the willow trees.

Rain kisses me in broad daylight.
Rain's lips are wet with strawberry juice.

Rain sings a quiet song,
Ushering a balmy twilight.

Rain never tells us where she sleeps.
Jane, when we light the candle
And sit down together,

Rain bickers outside the window
Deep into the night.
At last in the morning
She goes away somewhere.

by Man-yung Chang

THE FERRY BOAT AND THE PASSENGER

I am a ferry boat.
You're my passenger.

You tread on me with muddy feet.
I cross the river, hugging you in my arms.

When you are in my arms,
I do not care
Whether the river is deep, shallow or rapid.

If you do not come,
I wait for you from morning till night,
Exposed to winds and wet with snow or rain.

Once you reach the other bank,
You go away without looking back.
But I know you will come back some day.
So I grow old, waiting for you day and night.

I am a ferry boat.
You're my passenger.

by Yong-woon Han

PRELUDE

Let me have no shame
Under the heaven
Till I die.

Even winds among the foliage
Pained my heart.

With a heart that sings of the stars,
I'll love all dying things.

And I must fare the path
That's been allotted to me.

Tonight also
The winds sweep over the stars.
                    by Dong-ju Yun

BOY

Everywhere the sad autumn drops like maple leaves,
yielding its place to the spring. The sky
spreads beyond the branches. As I gaze at the sky,
a blue pigment dyes my eyebrows. When I touch
my warm cheeks, a blue dye stains my palms.
I look at the palms again. A clear stream
flows along the palm-lines, reflecting a face
sad as love—fair Suny's face. Enraptured,
I close my eyes. The clear stream still
reflects the face sad as love—fair Suny's face.
                    by Dong-ju Yun

DO YOU KNOW THAT DISTANT COUNTRY?

Mother, do you know that distant country?

Beyond the thick forest
white sea birds hover over a calm lake;
in narrow lanes wild roses are red,
and little calves freely frolic about.
Do you know that distant country
Where no one dwells?

When you go to that country,
Please do not forget;
Let us go together
and breed doves there.

Mother, do you know that distant country?

Below the gentle mountain slopes,
white goats idly graze
on the sunny field.
Among the tall cornstalks
the sun is setting.
The melancholy sounds
of the waves come from the distant ocean.
Do you know that distant country
where no one dwells?

Mother, please do not forget;
Let us return home with our little calves.

Mother, do you know that distant country?

Doves fly far and high in May's sky.
When it rains like today,
the pheasants will sing leisurely and
the autumn crows will soar high;
wild chrysanthemums will be more lovely and
yellow ginko leaves will gently dance in the
blue sky.

Mother, when in that country in the autumn
honey-bees buzz in the sunny orchards,
won't you pick the red apples with me?
                                    by Suk-jung Shin

SONGBOOK DOVES

When the mountain areas of Songbook District
    acquired new addresses,
The doves who had inhabited the hills
    lost their old home.
The early morning explosions at the quarry
Made them scared and sick at heart.
Under the blue morning sky resembling God's garden,
The doves still circled Songbook District,
Perhaps conveying blessings to the residents.
Among the dry, dreary ravines of the district
There was not even a large enough garden
Where they could feed in peace.
Each place they went echoed with the explosions
    at the quarry.
They sought refuge on rooftops,
Feeling homesick in the early morning
    with coal smoke from the chimneys.
At last they went back to the quarry
To warm their bills with stones just dug out.
These birds of love and peace,
Who revered man as a saint and lived in peace with him,
Have now lost man and mountain.
They have become hunted birds,
Unable even to conceive thoughts of love or peace.

by Kwang-sup Kim

BLUE BIRDS

When I die,
I'll become a blue bird.

I'll fly over
Blue sky and blue field.

I'll sing blue songs
And blue laments.

When I die,
I'll become a blue bird.
            by Ha-woon Han

COUNTING THE STARS

The autumn fills the sky
where seasons flow.

Carefree, I think I can count
all the stars in the autumn sky.
But I cannot count all the stars
that come to mind one after another
because the morning will soon come,
because I still have tomorrow night,
because my youth is not yet done.

one star and memory
one star and love
one star and solitude
one star and longing
one star and poetry
one star and Mother, Mother

Mother, I say one beautiful word for each star.
The names of childhood classmates; names of
foreign girls like Ling, Peng; names of
girls who are mothers now; names of my poor
neighbours; dove, puppy, rabbit, mule, deer;
names of poets like Francis Jammes and Rainer
Maria Rilke.

But they are too far away like the distant stars.
And, Mother, you are in distant Manchuria.

Longing for something, I write my name
on this star-lit hill, and then cover it with earth.
The insects chirping all night through
bemoan their shameful names.

When the winter passes and the spring comes to my star,
the grass will proudly cover
the hill where my name is buried,
as green turf grows on the tombs.

by Dong-ju Yun

THE TRUTH ABOUT THE INCIDENT

Darkness and the boiler...
The darkness was the sole cause for the failure to fathom
    the shapes of things
I laid the body that had hardened among human beings
On the sloping side of the boiler
And I indulged in a dialogue with the constellations

The rising wails of the high-voltage currents
penetrated the spine like the night's phosphorescence
the crumbling lives and the snowy dawns of the last days
The hazy tints of ammonia
rising at the climar of pleasure-seeking
The sea and the sky with swollen lungs and the
    approaching 25th hour

Rays of light: "Closely watch the ends of all destinies."
The cries of the chief engineer echoed by fellow
    technicians
And loud explosions

In the brilliance of arc-lamps
the poet experiences the premonitions with naked eyes
The boiler had numberless glands of despair
resembling capillary vessels

Death and the corpses, and the Poet has fallen
with burnt hair and severed limbs
the sun's music and the sea's radiance
O, the new sea's rays and the sun's music start to flow
"Nothing has ever happened."

by Kyu-dong Kim

PART FOUR

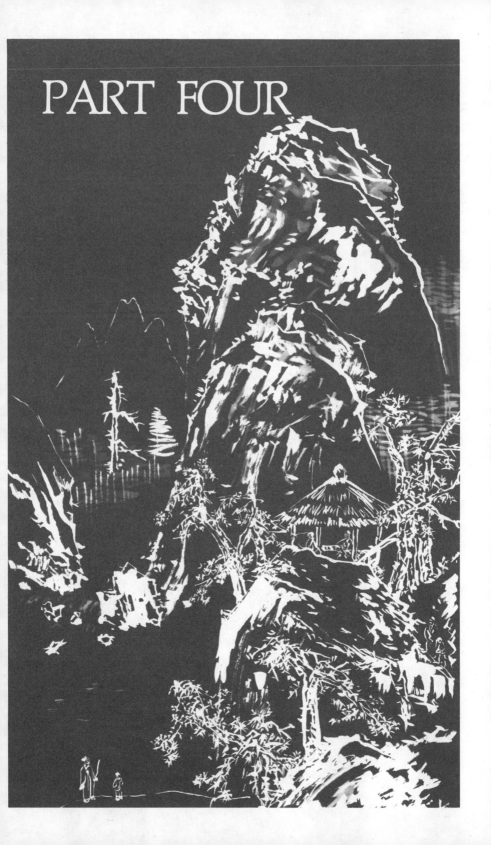

PRAYER IN AUTUMN

In the autumn
Let me pray...
Fill me with my humble mother-tongue
That you have given me
For the season of dead leaves.

In the autumn
Let me love...
Let me choose the one person in the world.
Let me tend this fertile season
For the fairest fruit.

In the autumn
Let me be alone...
Let my soul resemble the crow
That flew over the billowing sea
And the vale of lilies
To perch on this bare branch.

by Hyun-sung Kim

MEMORY

One, two, three... days
I strolled the seashore
to forget thóse days.

Summer, fall, winter
and by this wintry sea
where sea-women no longer
dive for seashells.

One, two, three... days
I strolled the seashore
to forget those days.
                    by Byung-hwa Cho

SUNLIGHT WHISPERING TO STONE-WALL

I want to gaze at the skies all day long,
Lying quiet on Spring's path;
Like sunrays whispering to a stone-wall,
Like a smiling stream underneath the grasses.

I want to gaze at the silken sky
Where a soft emerald-stream flows
Like shyness on a maiden cheek,
Like the ripples that caress Poesy's bosom.
                                    by Yung-rang Kim

TO MY BEDCHAMBER

Madonna! now the night, weary of all the feasts,
    will soon retire.
Ah, you must rush to me before the dawn breaks,
With dewdrops on your peach breasts.

Madonna! leave behind all the pearls of your family
That have been inherited eye to eye.
Come with your body alone, let's make haste.
We are two stars that must hide somewhere
    when the day breaks.

Madonna! in the soul's dark, deserted streets,
I am waiting, trembling with fear.
Ah, the first cock crows and the dogs bark!
My maiden, do you too hear?

Madonna! let's go to the bedchamber
That I polished all through the night-tide.
The old moon is about to sink and my ears hear footfalls.
O are you coming, my maiden?

Madonna! look at my soul's candle flicker and pine;
It will suffocate even in a downy breeze
And disperse like thin smoke.

Madonna! come, let us depart.
The mountain shadow is approaching stealthily.
Ah, someone will see us, my heart leaps.
I am calling you, my maiden.

Madonna! the day is about to break. Come quickly.
Let your hands clasp my neck
Before the temple bells deride us.
Let us go to that eternal country with this night.

Madonna! there is none will open my bedchamber
Beyond the lone bridge of remorse and fear.
Ah, the winds arise. Come lightly like the wind.
Are you coming, my maiden?

Madonna! it's a pity, I must have gone mad.
For I hear unreal sounds. My soul and body are
Burning as if all my blood, all my soul's fount
        have gone dry.

Madonna! we could go there anytime. If we must,
Let us go willingly, not forced.
My Mary, you believe in my words.
You must know that my bedchamber is a sepulchre
        of resurrection.

Madonna! the dreams that Night offers,
The dreams we weave and the dreams of life
        that men dream;
They are not different but all alike.
Ah, let us go to my bedchamber, to that beautiful
        and eternal land
Innocent and free as children.

Madonna! the laughters of the stars are fading
And the dark night's waves are subsiding.
Ah, you must come before the fog disperses.
I am calling you, my maiden.
                              by Sang-hwa Lee

CUCKOO

Cuckoo, Cuckoo,
My sister who used to live
By *Jindu* River

Is now crying in the village
By *Jindu* River.

In the old days,
In the far-away vales,
My sister who was living
By *Jindu* River
Was killed by her step-mother's hate.

It saddens me to call her,
My sister who was killed by the hate
And became a cuckoo.

Her nine brothers
She could never forget,
Never forget.

In the dead of night
When the world is asleep,

She cries mournfully, flying
From hill to hill.

by So-wol Kim

LOVE'S SILENCE

Love has gone. Ah, my love has gone.
He has left, shaking me off, and breaking
the green mountain light along the small path
toward the maple grove. The old promise that
was firm and bright as golden flowers has been
carried away like cold dust by a breath of breeze.
The memory of the keen first kiss has receded,
changing my fate's course. Your sweet voice has
deafened me and your fair face has blinded me.

Love after all is a human affair; so I feared
our parting when we first met. But this parting
has been too sudden, and my surprised heart is
bursting with fresh sorrow. To make parting
a source of idle tears will only mar love itself.
So I have poured the hopeless sorrow into a keg
of new hope. As we dread parting when we meet,
so we believe in reunion when we part.

Ah, my love has gone, but I have not let him go.
A love-song that cannot bear its own music
hovers over the love's silence.

                    by Yong-woon Han

FALLING PETALS

I

Should the wind be blamed
For the falling petals?
The stars outside the bead-curtain
Fade away one after another.
The distant hills loom nearer
After the philomel's song.
I should blow out the candle
Now the petals are falling.
The shadows of falling flowers
Are cast upon the lawn,
And the white paper-door
Faintly flushes.
The hermit's gentle heart
Will be known to the world, I fear.
These petals falling at dawn
Make me cry.

II

Only the haloed candle-light knows
The tender and kind heart
That secretly blooms and falls.
The petals drop so quietly,
The listening will stifle the sound.
When the cuckoo has had his fill,
It saddens me so to be all alone.

by Ji-hoon Cho

ON THE THRESHOLD OF AUTUMN

On a windy evening
I listen
As the winds usher in the autumn;
The falling leaves moan by the window.
As I listen again,
Distant footfalls echo near.
I live the days, hidden like crabs,
And the nights half awake.
The autumn inhabits my night, too;
Cold frost gathers on an empty mind.

by Gon-kang Yun

HAZE

A dim voice calls
From a distant field.
But I can see no one
In the fine haze.
Another call comes
Dimly from far away.

by Gon-kang Yun

SENSES OF LIFE

The bells of the dawn ring;
The morning stars twinkle;
Men live together.

The cocks crow;
The dogs bark.
Men come and go;
Come toward me,
Go away from me.

The sky has fallen in pain;
The green light has gone to the wild
Over the dark, flooded river.

I stood alone on a crumbling dike;
Sunplants were in full bloom,
Shaking the senses of life.

by Kwang-sup Kim

FROM MEMORY

I wake from a daytime slumber.
The electric light is flooding the room.
I hear merry laughing voices
    from somewhere afar,
Though I can see no one around.
I look to where the sounds come from.
My family are sitting around the dinner table.
But the distance seems as great
As between here and that other world.
I shout at the top of my voice, but
No one turns his head.
What a wall divides them from me!
I make a begging call to Mother.
My voice only returns futilely
Like a mountain echo.

Suddenly fear and sorrow seize me;
I burst out crying,
Gazing at the dull electric bulb.
Mother, Mother!
I learn at last life's sorrow.
Tears gather to my eyes.

by Yun-sung Kim

THE AUTUMN RIVER GLOWING WITH LAMENTATION

When my heart is restless,
I follow a friend's sorrowful love story
Through the autumn sunlight.
At last we reach the mountain ridge,
And tears come to my eyes.

The lantern light gathered at the elder brother's house
On the day of ancestral rites!
But I see the autumn river at sunset
Glowing with lamentation.

Look! Look!
Neither you nor I....
The stream's voice has ceased
In the valley of my first love's joy.
The sorrow of the next love has melted, too.

And now the river nears the sea
With a maddening story.
I see for the first time
The autumn river with a hushed voice.

by Jae-sam Park

IN THE AUTUMN

A leaf quietly wafts through the autumn
Gleaming with bright sunlight.
Let me believe that with bright smiles
We can shore up this huge earth.

Let us find you
In the ripples of the bell sounds;
In the tiny, hard grip of the baby
Clinging to its mother's skirt.

There will never come a day
When all our yesterdays and todays
Are buried irretrievably in legends.

Today I want to believe an eternal truth
Grandmother's words that the moon has a cinnamon tree
To be cut out with a silver hatchet.

In the burning sickbed of my childhood
I was falling in a bottomless abyss.
That endless, headlong fall caused me
To pass out again and again.
Let us protect our dear dreams
From that terrible truth.

by Han-mo Chung

THREE QUATRAINS

The odor of the lotus lady I meet in dreams
And that of my wife are similar at times.
But I don't know which is more true,
The love I give or the love I take in dreams and awake.

☆   ☆   ☆

My friend, as if lying in a water-soaked coffin,
On days when we suffer for a woman,
Let us go to the sea and become
Grass leaves on the blue waves.

☆   ☆   ☆

How many would know
How to prepare the bridal bed in the other world?
But all my dreams in previous lives were to meet a woman
To whom I could give even the agonies deep in my soul.

by Woo-shik Kang

BLIND ALLEY

In the blind alley
Where a dark dog barks darkly
A withered leaf scrapes
Against the cheeks of an old man
Selling chestnuts in the corner.

From the windswept backlane where
Aging windows are closed tightly,
The distant sky looks very narrow.
In the eyes of the old man reflecting the sky,
The large typefaces of a newspaper are crumpled.
And a newspaper boy shouts into the alley.

On an autumn evening smelling of fresh chestnuts,
The street noises groan hoarsely.
In the backlane where the dark dog stalks,
A dreadful silence reigns.

by Tae-jin Park

THE VACUUM CONFERENCE

Leaning over a wall made up of numberless hanged corpses,
moving skulls and women's blue pelves,
the watchman recites Chapter III, St. Matthew.
Dr. Freud wearing a white gown and a white mask
comes up the stairs with nurse Curie.
The temperature is normal, being zero."
I attended the emperor's wedding in a hearse the first day
The next day I violated a woman in a first-class coach
The next day I swallowed a coffee pot
On the last afternoon I attempted to kill myself
by falling from the tall university building
Miss Curie, please prepare for an amputation operation."
Is there no hope, Dr. Freud?"
Dr. Freud climbs up the staircase after nurse Curie
Above his head
Only glittering outbursts of laughter resembling
Glasses breaking against granite columns

by Kyu-dong Kim

BACKGROUND

Though I close my eyes again and again
Till I can see the distant heavens,
I can't see what is invisible.
Though barefoot I may wander all night,
Lie on the right side and then turn to the left,
I can't rush to the sea fifteen miles away
And put her to sleep.

Wave chasing wave
Wind chasing wind
The dream dreamless like a corpse's.

Even if a bone I threw away last fall
Hides its body in the sand field
Or luckily becomes crab spittle,
What would it mean at all?
The sky is deep, and
Our sleep under the sky is heavy.

                              by Un-kyo Kang

VIEW FROM THE WINDOW

Morning
A thousand pigeons fly into the riverside church,
And disappear in the space inside.
Boats on the river shove into my room,
Flooding it with water and submarine light.

Afternoon
In the deserted public park
An old man buries himself in Sunday papers.
Stray winds casually caress
The sun's rays sifting through leaves.
And pigeons fondly linger about his feet,
Pecking at the silvery sounds
From the nearby church's chimes.

Evening
The lanterns in the public park
Flicker on like poignant reminders.
I have seen airplanes desperately defying time,
Chasing shadows that quickly devour
Miles of land and town.
But time here devoutly pauses
Under the leafless trees.

As I turn off the light,
Irrelevant images fall among bare branches
Like imaginary flower petals:
A woman drawing water out of a well
Where gloden light gushes out;
A thousand fish eyes staring in the dark;
And dark wings fluttering in the darkness.

by Chang-soo Koh

PART FIVE

PART FIVE

LANDSCAPE

The ivy is green along the forest path;
The river gleams among the trees.

Wild birds perch on sun-lit boughs;
The white clouds saunter in the sky.

Crow-songs overflow the valley, and
The winds rush over the hills.

The streamlet is clear as jade
Beyond the winding forest paths.

The green mountains will live for a thousand years;
The river will flow for ten thousand
In this painted landscape....

by Suk-jung Shin

NONGAE, WHO DIED FOR HER COUNTRY

The noble indignation
Fiercer than religious faith;
The burning passion
Stronger than love.

O, a soul redder than poppies flowed
On waves bluer than cornflower.

The fair eye-lashes trembled;
The pomegranate lips kissed Death.

O, a soul redder than poppies flowed
On waves bluer than cornflower.

The flowing river will remain forever blue;
The beautiful soul will remain forever red.

O, a soul redder than poppies flowed
On waves bluer than cornflowers.

by Yung-ro Byun

FLOWERS ON THE HILLS

Flowers bloom, bloom
In the hills.
Autumn, Spring, Summer
Flowers bloom.

The flowers blooming
In the hills yonder
Are there all, all alone.

The little birds singing in the hills
Dwell in the hills
For the love of flowers.

Flowers fall, fall
In the hills.
Autumn, Spring, Summer
Flowers fall.

by So-wol Kim

HILLS SURROUND ME

The hills surround me, and
Tell me to live my life,
Sowing the seeds,
Tilling the land.

Build a house below a hill,
Bear sons, bear daughters;
Plant pumpkins along the mud walls.
Live like wild roses,
Live like wormwood.

The hills surround me, and
Tell me to live like clouds,
Tell me to live like winds;
Life will soon wane like the moon!

by Mok-wol Park

BLUE DAYS

On dazzling blue days
Let us long for the loved ones.

The autumn flowers have fallen and
The tarnished green is tinted by maples.

What if it snows?
What if the spring returns?
If I die and you live!
If you die and I live!

by Jung-ju Suh

THE MOON, GRAPES, LEAVES

Suny! the moonlight is flooding
The antique garden
Where insects are chirping.

The moon quietly sits in my garden;
The moon is more fragrant than fruit.

The autumn night
Blue
Like the East Sea.

Grapes are lovely, wet with moonlight;
Grapes feed on moonlight.

Suny! the young leaves
Beneath the twining vines
Look lonely, wet with moonlight.
                    by Man-yung Chang

BUDDHIST DANCE

The white silken hood
Soft as a butterfly.

The bluish shaven head
Hidden in the silk hood.

The light tinging the cheeks
Is fair sorrowfully.

The candles quietly melt and
The moon wanes on every paulownia leaf.

The long sleeves shroud the wide sky,
The seed-shaped shoes move as in flight.

The dark eyes rise
To gaze at a star.

The two pearls on the peach-cheeks.
Though weary of the world,
Agony is a starlight.

The arms fold and then stretch
Like devout hands in prayer.

The crickets chirp away the night
And the white silken hood
Is soft as a butterfly.

by Ji-hoon Cho

DOES SPRING COME TO A LOST LAND

Now someone else's land... does Spring come
    to a usurped land?
Bathed all over in sunlight, I saunter as in a dream
Along the straight paddy-field path
To where the blue sky and the green field meet.
Silent sky and field! I have not come here alone.
Did you lure me? Or did someone call?
Please answer, I implore.
The wind whispers into my ears,
Pulling my sleeves to urge me on.
The larks are laughing behind the clouds
Like maidens hidden in the grove.

Fertile wheat fields! the gentle rain that started
After midnight has made your hair glow like hemp.
My hair feels so light, too.
Let me rush ahead, though all alone.
The kind ditches around the dry paddy-fields
Are singing lullabies as to a suckling babe,
Dancing in glee all alone.

Butterflies, swallows! do not hurry.
I must say hello to the cockscomb village, too.
I want to see that field the nameless maiden
        used to weed.

Let me take a hoe in my hand.
I will tread this soil tender as a plump breast
Till my ankles ache. I want to shed much sweat.
My soul races, free and boundless
Like children by the river-side.
What are you looking for? Where are you going?
It's strange, please answer.

My whole body smells of fresh greens.
I walk all day long, limping between green laughter
        and green sorrow.
I must be under Spring's spell.
But now the land is another's.
And Spring will be usurped, too, I fear.

                                by Sang-hwa Lee

INTERFUSION

As the day sets silently into a stone,
A naked poplar tree comes into view
With similar motion.

There is not a whiff of wind
To shake the gathering perspective.

As I look up the splendour, the fruit,
And the all-embracing vines,
The treetop recedes into the distance
And becomes the sky.

by Han-mo Chung

CHUANG-TZE'S POEM NO. 7

A pair of scissors carve out fresh fish figures
An esprit shakes off its scales
A pair of compasses draws the full moon
The fine gauze catches the moonlight
I photograph sunlight breathing in a vitamin ampule
A red sun rises out of the sea
Objects dance in my old-fashioned camera
An ancient sword hangs on the wall
The sea is ill on the flashing sword-blade.

by Je-chun Park

BIRCH TREE

I have seen a French Impressionist exhibition. There was
a snowy landscape. A woman was knitting in a quiet
garden where sunlight poured down. Trees reflected in
the water. A daughter hugged in her mother's arms.
The Seine flowed. Let them be. In the garden in front of
the gallery, a birch tree quietly trembles in full bloom.
A few branches shiver whitely.

by Yung-gul Lee

WINDOW WHERE THE AFTERNOON FLOWS IN

The walls were broken in the garden.
The windows staring into the street
Gleamed all day with a dismal counter current.

On that afternoon, shadows were cast
Over cleavages in the wall
In the city center where darker shadows flickered.

The broken walls and the washlines
Quietly disturbed the skies.
A shrill voice came from afar
And the roar of automobiles rebuked our hopes.
The afternoon basked in the warm sunshine.

For a while I was covered with death's ashes.
In the city center old concepts were trodden down
On such serene afternoons.

Water flowed from a broken faucet.
The windows that stared into the street
Could be seen in the distance
Reflecting a host of glances.

by Tae-jin Park

A SPRING DAY

The city walks into the grass leaves.
The children of the sleeping city
Take the elevator of grass leaves
And rapidly descend into the earth.

The widest road lies in the roots,
In your roots.
                              by Un-kyo Kang

EVENING WIND

I strike matches again and again,
But the darkness does not go away.
I fall down again and again,
But death does not come near.
An evening wind only passes
Through the forest burnt to ashes.
                              by Un-kyo Kang

CHUANG-TZE'S BUTTERFLY

As I write poetry in the middle of night,
Chuang-tze's butterfly hangs on the wall.
He sends me an insinuating glance.
Since when?
The butterfly I could only meet in dreams
Flutters his soft wings in my landscape.
From what depths has he come,
His wings dripping with dewdrops?
He is steeped in green mountain shade.
It is perhaps to sharpen my poetic vision
That this butterfly makes eyes at me.
Chuang-tze's butterfly who smells of the lush woods
And gives glimpses of Chuang-tze's spare beard.

                              by Chang-soo Koh

THE BUTTERFLY'S JOURNEY

My baby each night starts on a journey,
Stirring the night's darkness with its soft wings,
Flying across Slumber's stream,
Over Memory's brilliant meadows,
And against Tomorrow's surging sea.
At last it hits a pitch-dark cliff or a labyrinth,
And returns home frightened.

As I open a dark book-cover,
Gunpowder smell mixes with infernal cries.
War ceaselessly smolders there,
In the light violet veil of fog;
The blue terror's river ends there.
Love is a blue-bird on its wings;
Encounter always brings mutual anxiety;
Even dreams cannot arrest longing.

My baby at last returns from dreamland
And in my arms folds its weary wings,
Dripping with dream dewdrops.
In which windswept valley, my baby,
Did a ferocious eagle frighten you tonight?

by Han-mo Chung

JOURNEY

Though you may hang dreams
On dreary boughs like blossoms,

From the hills the mother is gone,
And the daughter is picking acorns
Which her mother has left unpicked.

When I visit your home village,
I can no more find you there;
Only the skies remain.

Bleak autumn.
I roll up crumpled expressions
Like faded pictures hanging
In a lonely house on lease.

The waning revolution.
Ah, I have grown old amid wars!
                            by Sul-joo Lee

RIVER VILLAGE

I

From the distance, the mountains look deserted, green and
hushed. As I near the hills and climb slowly, I see a silent
waterfall, a sharp rock hewn by water, and leaves
waving in the wind. The voices of mountain birds mix
with the sounds of water. And azaleas are in full bloom
on a steep cliff.

II

Ridge after gentle ridge all around. Between this hill
and that, a blue river flows. The quiet stream comes
around the bend and reaches that bend way below.
Forsythia on the mountain-side, azalea on the precipice,
this beautiful spring day quietly flows. People call
this village River Village, but this is the only fairy
land possible. The river only gently runs, but at the
same time it connects with others. So this spring day it
creates a sense of eternity. It generates a full sense
of eternity on this spring day.

by Yung-gul Lee

BRONZE LAW

A flame drawn from the depths of slumber
Jumps over the fence to another world
Leaving only its ashes.
I spend days all alone
Lost in the fun of watching.

by Je-chun Park

RABBIT HUNTING NO. 7

In an old faded photograph
I see my childhood face
With a big gaping mouth.
I can see no eyes, no nose or ears;
My naked body leans on a barbwire fence
With a big gaping mouth
Desperately stretching a hand toward you
O my childhood face!

by Je-chun Park

About the Poets

Byun, Yung-ro 변 영 로 (1889-1961) wrote poetry in Korean and in English. He was one of the forerunners of modern poetry in Korea. Collections of his poems include: Korea's Mind, 1924; Azaleas (in English), 1945. He also published literary essays.

Chang, Man-yung 장 만 영 (1914-1976) wrote modernist poems in the 1930s. His publications of poetry include: Lamb, 1937; Festival, 1939; Song of Childhood, 1947; Night's Lyricism, 1956; Evening Bell, 1957; Collected poems of Chang Man-yung, 1964. He also translated foreign poetry into Korean.

Cho, Byung-hwa 조 병 화 (1921-   ) is a very prolific, and popular, poet with a large bulk of published poetry. He has written many memorable poems in plain Korean. His poetry books include: An Undesirable Heritage, 1949; One Day's Comfort, 1950; Man's Lonely Isle, 1954; Before Love Departs, 1955; People Who Wait, 1959; Night's Tale, 1961; At Low Voice, 1962; Between Dust and Wind, 1972. He has won several literary awards.

Cho, Ji-hoon 조 지 훈 (1920-1968) was a forerunner of modern Korean poetry and importantly contributed to Korean verse with several books of poems to his credit. He was a great lover of nature. His books of poetry include: Mountain Rain, 1930; Blue Deer Poems, 1946; Grass Leaves, 1952; Selected Poems of Cho Ji-hoon, 1956.

Cho, Yun-hyun 조 연 현 (1920-1983) was a major literary critic with many works of criticism to his credit. He was also editor of literary magazines. "Azalea Flowers" is one of the small number of poems he wrote.

Choe, Nam-sun 최 남 선 (1890-1957) was a champion of new cultural movements. He established the first magazine in Korea, and compiled and edited the first personal collection of Sijo poems.

Chu, Yo-han 주 요 한 (1900-1979) was a forerunner of the New Poetry Movement. Collections of his poems include: Beautiful Dawn, 1924; Peach Blossoms, 1919; Fireworks, 1919.

Chun, Bong-gun 전 봉 건 (1928-   ) has written many volumes of poetry and literary criticism. Collections of his poetry include: Repetitions for Love, 1959; In Search of Poetry, 1962; Chunhyang's Lovesong, 1967; Sea Within, 1970. He has won the Poets Association Award.

Chung, Han-mo 정 한 모 (1923-   ) is a leading contemporary poet. He has published several volumes of poetry and a few books of literary criticism. He is a professor of Korean literature at Seoul National University. His poetry is generally marked by clarity of meaning, and lucid imagery. His poems often show a devout attitude about life and a strong humanism. Collections of his poetry include: Chaos, 1950; Lyricism for Blank Space, 1959; Baby's Room, 1970. He has published critical studies including A Study of Modern Writers (1959). He has won the Modern Literature Award.

Ham, Hyung-soo 함 형 수 (1916-1946) has left behind a small number of poems. He is often remembered for his decadent tendency in his poetry.

Han, Ha-woon 한 하 운 (1919-1975) wrote many poems about the misery caused by leprosy to which he had fallen victim in his 20s. His poems were published in Selected Poems of Han Ha-woon, 1948; Grass Flute, 1957, and A Dirt Road, 1960.

Han, Yong-woon 한 용 운 (1879-1944), the famous Buddhist priest-patriot, wrote many poems which are among the best loved Korean poems. Among others, his poetry often reveals flashes of Buddhist insights into the inexplicable and paradoxical nature of existence. His poems were collected in Love's Silence, 1926. He also wrote novels.

Hwang, Sun-won 황 순 원 (1915-   ) has written a large number of short stories and novels and is an outstanding writer. He has also published poems in magazines and poetry books. He has received various literary awards.

Kang, Un-kyo 강 은 교(1945-   ) is prominent among the younger group of poets. A poignant awareness of the fragility of existence seems to permeate her poems. She often uses subtle language which organically fuses imagery, sense and sound. Her poetry is said to contain elements of shamanism, which seems quite likely. Her books of poems include: Nihilism, Grass Leaves, and The Diary of the Poor. She has also published prose writing.

Kang, Woo-shik 강 우 식 (1941-   ) occupies a peculiar place among the contemporary poets. Among other things, he has nearly confined his poetic utterances to "quatrains." Much of his poetry is said to echo the traditional tone color and rhythms of Korean verse. Many of his quatrains demonstrate his skill in amalgamating words into excellent metaphor and imagery. Collections of his poems include: Quatrains, 1974; Snow-storms of Koryo, 1977; As I Began Picking Flowers, 1979. He won the Modern Literature Award in 1974.

Kim, Chun-soo 김 춘 수 (1922-   ) has prominently contributed to Korean poetry and literary criticism, which has received recognition through various literary distinctions. One might say that he has had a large share in adding the variegated tints of the Western canvas to the oriental painting of traditional Korean poetry. His poems are marked, among others, by excellent visual imagery and a delicate sensitivity. Collections of his poems include: Cloud and Rose, 1948; Swamp, 1950; Flag, 1951; Death of a Girl in Budapest, 1959.

Kim, Dong-hwan 김 동 환 (1901-   ) is widely known for his epic poems. Collections of his poems include: Night at the Frontier, 1925; Ascending Youth, 1926; Wild Rose, 1942. He at one time edited the literary magazine, The Three Thousand Miles.

Kim, Dong-myung 김 동 명 (1901-1968) wrote many poems on patriotic, religious and philosophic themes. His books of poetry include: Plantain, 1938; My Mind, 1964; 38th Parallel, 1947; Pearl Harbour, 1955. He won the Free Literature Award in 1954.

Kim, Hyun-sung 김 현 승 (1913-1981) set a major milestone in the country's literary history with many remarkable poems. Some of his poems contain excellent visual imagery. His poetry is also marked by a devoutness perhaps of the Christian faith and a vision which sees things through to their intrinsic nature. His books of poems include: Selected Poems of Kim Hyun-sung, 1957; Defender's Song, 1963; Solid Solitude, 1968; Absolute Solitude, 1970.

Kim, Jong-han 김 종 한 (1916-1944) was one of the champions of the Pure Poetry Movement and wrote several poems reminiscent of folksongs. His books of poetry include Like Apricot Blossoms, 1940. "A Landscape with an Old Well" is a favorite poem.

Kim, Kwang-kyun 김 광 균 (1913-   ) was one of the leaders of the Korean Modernist Movement, introducing modernist techniques in his poetry. Some of his poems are noted for excellent visual imagery. Collections of his poetry include: Gaslight, 1939; Port of Call, 1947; Twilight Song, 1957.

Kim, Kwang-sup 김 광 섭 (1905-1977) wrote many volumes of poetry which came to place him among the major poets of this country. His poetry shows an unusual skill in capturing the essential qualities of things with lucid and concrete imagery. Collections of his poems include: Longing, 1938; Mind, 1949; Sunflower, 1957; Songbook District Doves, 1966; Reaction, 1971. He won the Seoul City Cultural Award in 1958.

Kim, Kyu-dong 김 규 동 (1923-   ) spearheaded the Korean modernist poetic movement in the 1950s. He has also contributed to literary criticism. The poet himself admits to surrealist influences on his poetry. His poems often depict war-torn "mind-scapes." His

poetry includes: Butterfly and Plaza and Modern Myth, 1918. He
has also published books of criticism including New Poetic Theory,
1959, and Study of Modern Poetry, 1970.

Kim, Nam-jo 김 남 조 (1927-　　) has written many poems on
Christian themes. Her collections of poetry include: Life, 1951, Tree
and Wind, 1958; Maple Woods, 1963; Soul and Bread, 1973. She
won the Free Literature Award in 1958.

Kim, Sang-yong 김 상 용 (1902-1950) wrote several poems on
pastoral themes. His poems were carried in Nostalgia, published in
1935.

Kim, So-wol 김 소 월 (1902-1934) is perhaps more popular and
more widely read than any other modern Korean poet. In his poems
he largely draws on the rhythms and themes of Korean folk songs.
Naturally, and in an extraordinary way, his poetry strikes respon-
sive chords in the Korean heart. His poems were published in
Azaleas in 1925. Collected Poems of Kim So-wol was published
posthumously.

Kim, Yun-sung 김 윤 성 (1925-　　) is an important poet today. His
books of poetry include: Mountain Path Overlooking the Sea, 1958;
Foreboding, 1970; Elegy, 1973. He won the Korean Writers' Associa-
tion Award in 1956.

Kim, Yung-rang 김 영 랑 (1903-1950) wrote many beautiful poems
marked by melodious verses and lucid imagery which appeal to
Koreans. He excelled in turning colloquial language into superb
poetic diction, capturing poetic qualities in everyday expressions. He
stands among the prominent lyrical poets Korea has ever produced.
Collections of his poems include: Collected Poems of Kim Yung-
rang, 1935; Selected Poems of Kim Yung-rang, 1956.

Koh, Chang-soo 고 창 수 (1934-　　) has published two volumes of
poetry in Korean and a book of Korean poems translated into
English. He received the Modern Korean Literature Translation
Award in 1980.

Lee, Jang-hi 이 장 희 (1902-1928) lived between 1902 and 1928.
Even though the bulk of his writing is very small, he has been ac-
claimed for his poetic talent. He is said to have written some 20
poems before he took his own life in the prime of youth. His poems
were carried in Sanghwa and Kowol, 1951. He is best remembered
by the poem, "Spring is a Cat."

Lee, Sang 이 상 (1910-1937) wrote short stories and poems which
were often praised as the works of a genius and at other times de-

nounced as mere ravings. As in his personal life, he ignored or defied conventions in his writing. He was perhaps the first on the Korean literary scene to try his hand at Dadaist and Surrealist poetry with such boldness. His poems were carried in Crow's-eye-View, 1934. He also wrote novels including Wings, 1936.

Lee, Sang-hwa 이 상 화 (1900-1941) wrote several memorable poems which are among the most widely read and best-loved poems. He is best remembered by "To my Bedchamber" and "Does Spring Come to a Lost Land?" His poems were posthumously carried in Sang-hwa and Kowol, 1951.

Lee, Sul-joo 이 설 주 (1908-   ) started his poetic career in the 1920s, and has published several books of poems. Some of his poems give glimpses of traditional Korean rural scenes and speak with a typical Korean pathos. Collections of his poems include: Wild Chrysanthemum, Notes of a Wanderer, Chapter on Suffering, Chapter on Pathos, Gleanings of Life, and Thirty-six Years.

Lee, Yuk-sa 이 육 사 (1904-1944) left behind only 34 poems, which were collected posthumously in Poems of Yuk-sa, 1946. He wrote a number of patriotic poems and used modernistic techniques in his poetry.

Lee, Yung-gul 이 영 걸 (1939-   ) has published many volumes of poetry and literary criticism. He has also translated English poetry and criticism. He won the Modern Korean Literature Translation Award in 1972. His collections of poetry include: The Moon, 1974; Home-coming, 1976; This Wild Prairie, 1978; Concentrated Time, 1978.

No, Chun-myung 노 천 명 (1913-1957) has become one of the favorite poets with several books of poetry, which include: Coral Reefs, 1938; Windowside, 1945; Looking at the Stars, 1953; Deer's Song, 1956. She also published books of essays.

O, Il-do 오 일 도 (1901-1946) wrote several good poems. For some time he was editor of the Poetry Garden, a poetry magazine.

Park, Du-jin 박 두 진 (1916-   ) has written many excellent poems and has become a major poet. His collections of poems include: Visit to the Country, 1946; The Sun, 1949; Midday Prayer, 1953. He has also published books of literary criticism and essays. He received the Free Literature Award in 1956.

Park, In-hwan 박 인 환 (1926-1956) spearheaded Modern Poetry Movement and was a promising poet. He has left behind many well-loved poems. His demise at an early age was a great loss for the literary world. His poems were carried in the New City and the Citizen's Chorus, 1947, and Collected Poems of Park In-hwan, 1953.

Park, Jae-sam 박 재 삼 (1933-   ) has written many important poems and has become one of the best loved poets in this country to-day. It appears that he has been outstandingly successful in turning 'sorrow into beauty,' which has admittedly been one of his major concerns as a poet. Collections of his poems include: Chunhyang's Mind, 1962; In the Sunlight, 1970; Rain-swept Autumn Tree, 1980. He received the Modern Literature Award in 1957.

Park, Je-chun 박 제 천 (1945-   ) has published four books of poems and has won the Modern Literature Award for poetry. The bulk of his poetry is marked by what he terms "exercises in imagina-tion," which, often being exercises in fashioning novel and radical images, covers the worlds of Korean Buddhism and Korean classic literature. Collections of poetry include: Chuangtze's Poetry, 1975; Mind Method, 1979; Chuangtze's Poetry (revised), 1979. He won the Modern Literature Award in 1979.

Park, Mok-wol 박 목 월 (1916-1978) was among the forerunners of modern Korean poetry. He has left behind several outstanding volumes of poetry, marking a major landmark in Korean literary history. His life-long concern seems to have been with capturing and fostering the lyrical strain in the Korean language. Collections of his poetry include: Blue Deer Poems, 1946; Mountain Peach Blossoms, 1954; Orchids and Other Poems, 1959; Fallen Leaves in 1969. He has also published books of children's verse and literary essays. He received the Asia Free Literature Prize in 1955.

Park, Tae-jin 박 태 진 (1921-   ) has published several volumes of prose and poetry. The greater part of his poems describe urban scenes and commonplace things with the joys and frustrations of life in urban centers. His books of poetry include: Transformation, 1962; Love Story, 1969; and Each Day's Meaning, 1971.

Park, Yong-chul 박 용 철 (1904-1938) was a leader of the Pure Poetry Movement and wrote a considerable amount of lyric poetry. He also published literary magazines. His poems were carried in Complete Works of Park Yong-chul.

Shin, Dong-jip 신 동 집 (1924-   ) is a leading contemporary poet who has published several books of his poems. In interpreting real-ity, he has a peculiar way of restructuring it so that his poems illumi-nate commonplace things and events and endow them with hitherto unknown shapes and meanings. His collections of poems include: Banishment of Lyricism, 1952; Second Prologue, 1954; Water of Contradiction, 1963; Simmering Vowels, 1965; An Empty Coke

Bottle, 1968; Dawn Man, 1970; Return, 1971; Transmissions, 1973. He won the Free Asia Literature Award in 1955.

Shin, Suk-jung 신 석 정 (1907-1975) wrote many excellent poems on rural and pastoral themes. His collection of poetry includes: Candle Light, 1939; Sad Pastoral, 1947; Glacier, 1956; Mountain Overtures, 1967. He has also published translations of Chinese poems.

Suh, Jung-ju 서 정 주 (1915-   ) has made outstanding contributions to Korean poetry. His collections of poetry include: Flower Snake, 1941; Selected Poems of Suh Jung-ju, 1955; Notes on Silla, 1960; Complete Works of Suh Jung-ju, 1973. He has also published books of literary criticism and essays. He has received various literary awards.

Yang, Ju-dong 양 주 동 (1903-1977) was a prominent scholar of Korean literature and wrote important scholarly books of old Korean literature. His poems were carried in literary magazines and his collection of Poetry, Korea's Pulses, 1931.

Yu, Chi-hwan 유 치 환 (1908-1967) is a major poet with many memorable volumes of poetry to his credit. Collections of his poems include: Selected Poems of Chungma, 1939; Chapter on Life, 1947; Ullung Island, 1948; Ninth Collection of Poems, 1957. He won the Korean Poets Association Award, the Seoul City Cultural Award and the Free Literature Award.

Yun, Dong-ju 윤 동 주 (1917-1945) wrote many poems which have become favorite poems. He published his poems in The Sky, the Wind, the Stars and Poems, 1950.

Yun, Gon-kang 윤 곤 강 (1911-1949) published collections of poetry including Great Earth, 1937; Dirge, 1938; Glacier, 1940; Flute, 1948. He also wrote critical essays.